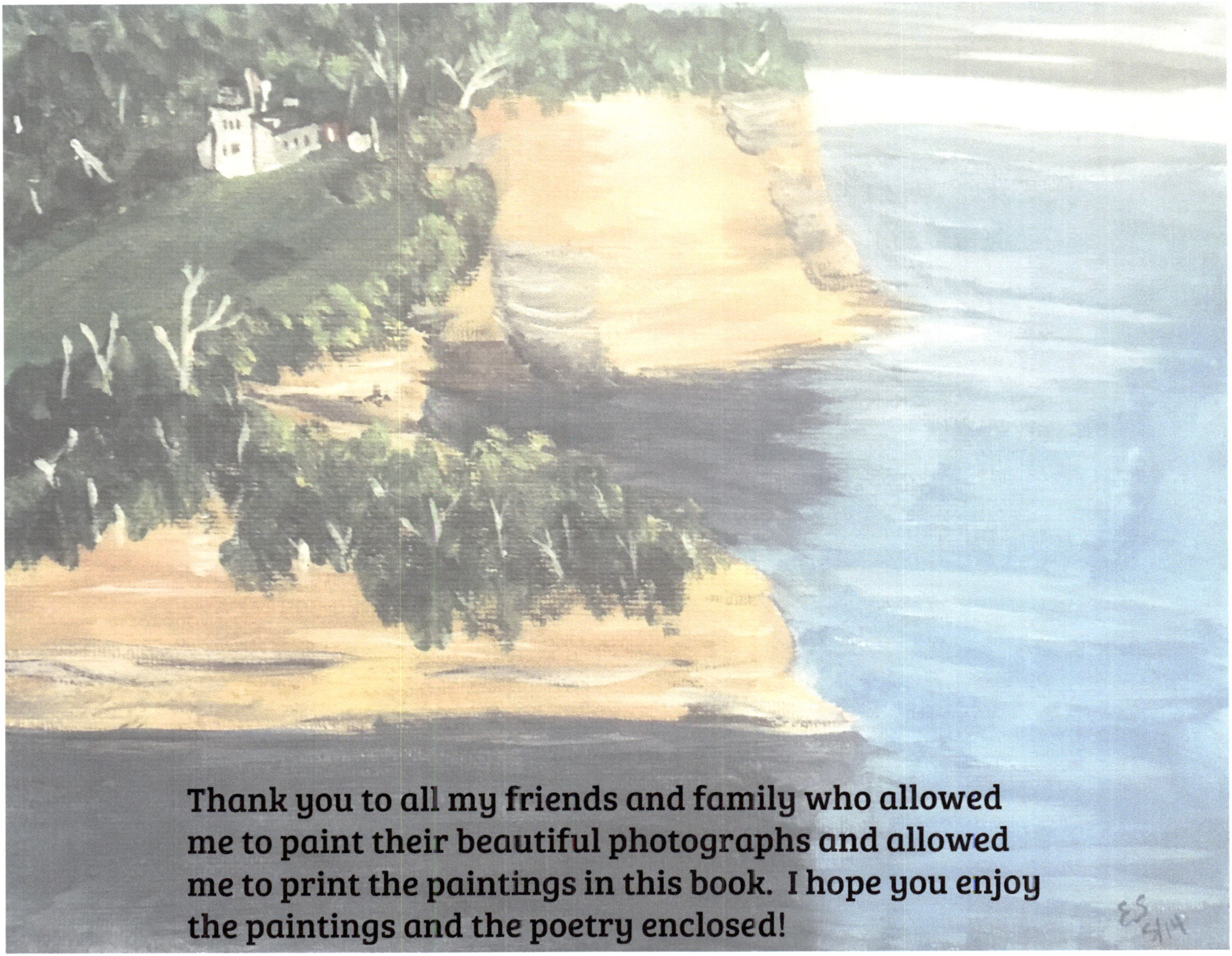

Thank you to all my friends and family who allowed me to paint their beautiful photographs and allowed me to print the paintings in this book. I hope you enjoy the paintings and the poetry enclosed!

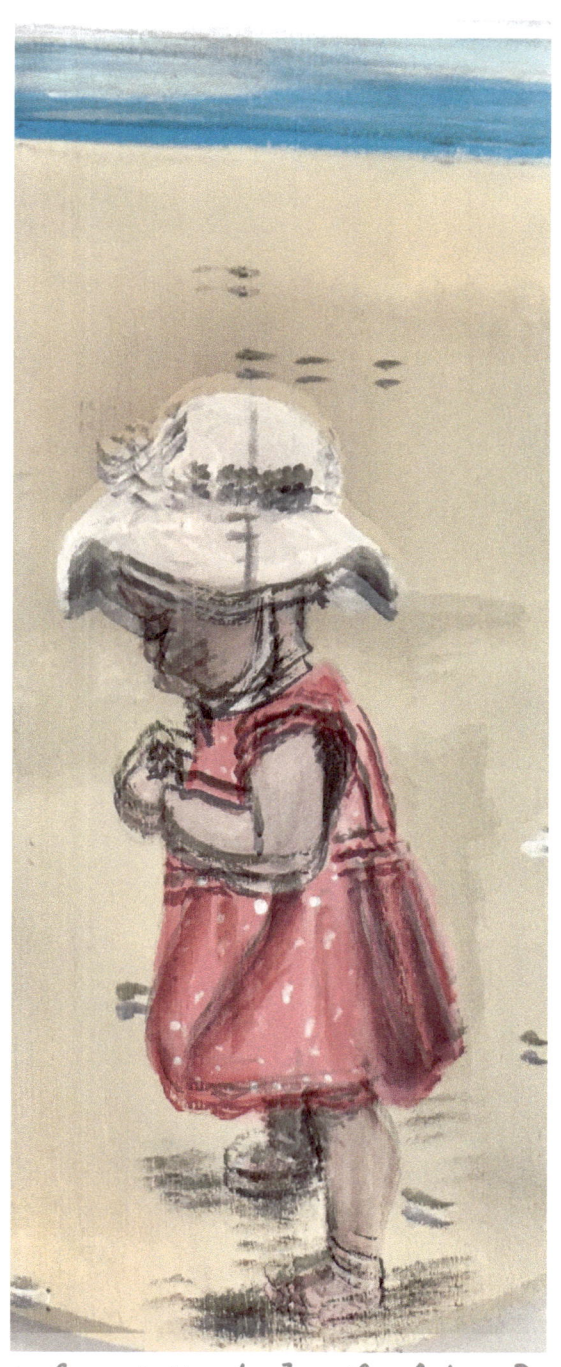

Photo for painting by Jennifer Arlene Pereira
of her daughter Sienna at Mrytle Beach, SC

Tomorrow's Warrior, Today's Cuddles

Sweet baby, the summer of my life. Your soft, chubby fingers are your curiosity's joy. In a world so hardened and bleak you fashion a wonderment. You are the harbinger of radiance. Sweet baby, you are a fire so fierce you will burn down walls. You are tomorrow's warrior but today you are loving cuddles and sticky kisses. Tomorrow you will make giant leaps but today we will rejoice as you toddle. Tomorrow you will conquer the world but today you will smile mischievously and conquer my heart.

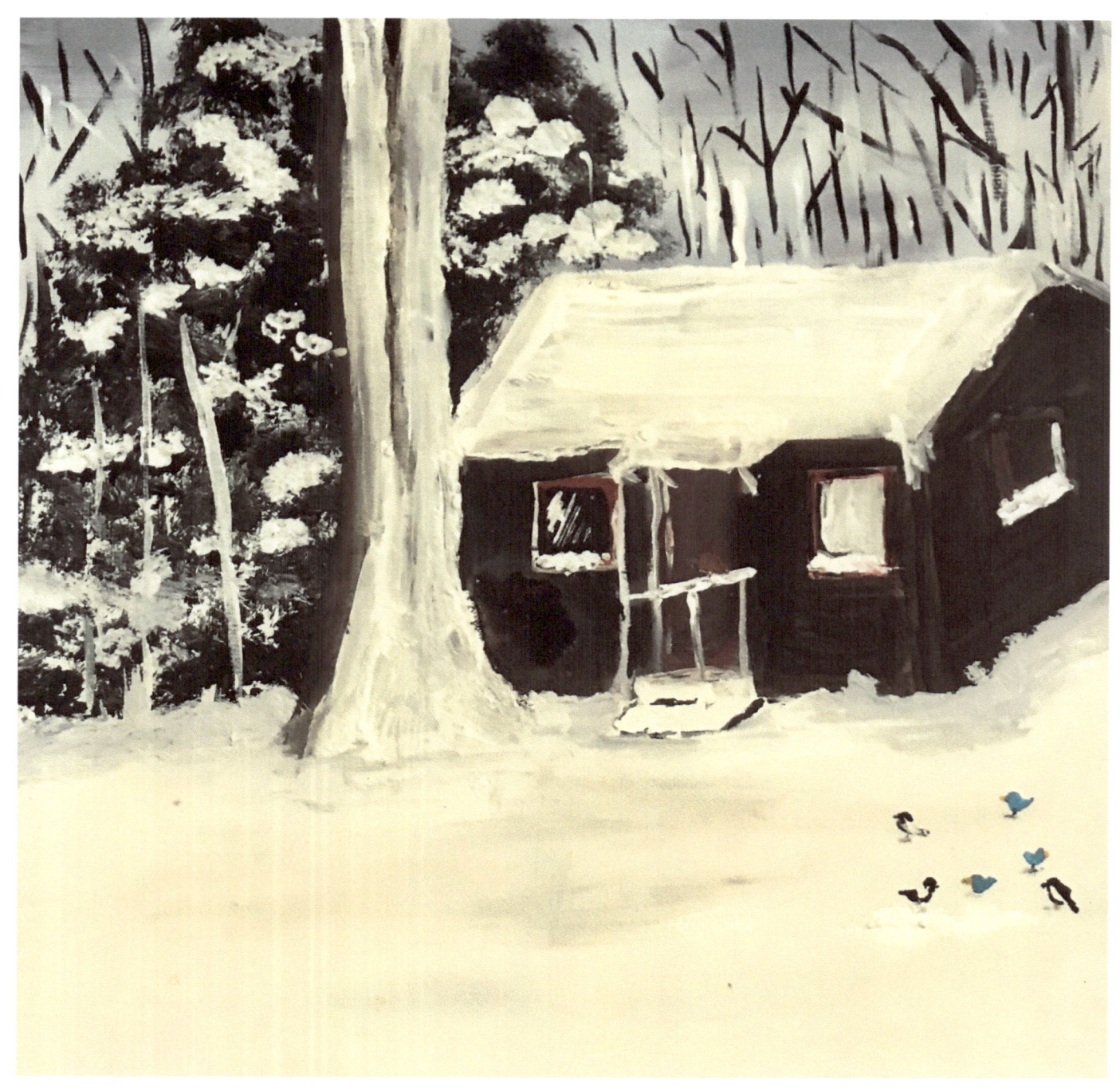

Photo for painting by Betty Perry
of the Shack in Baraga,, MI

The Shack

There's a little shack in the woods where memories live. It's not made of much, just a simple hovel. Happiness can be found there. Days bygone but not from the heart. Of family, of good times, of laughter, of tears. Merely sticks but such grandeur is unmatched. A winsome little shack in a northern wood. A treasure trove hid back in the sticks. A place of play, of growth, of ease. Just a plain, little shack but a mansion of affectionate nostalgia built to last forevermore.

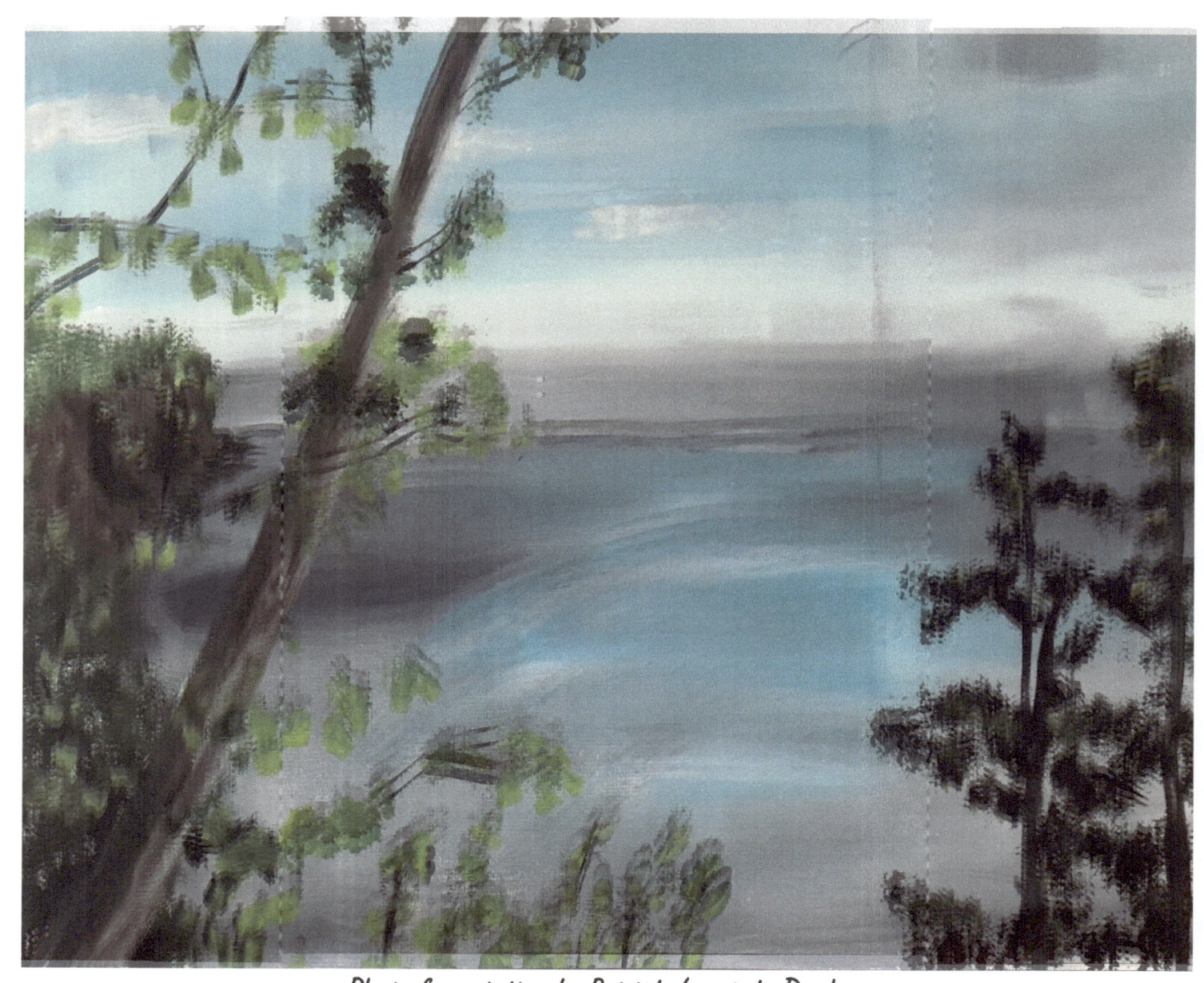

Photo for painting by Brigitte Lapointe-Dunham of the Presque Isle Park Marquette, MI

A Queen's Jewel

Tranquil sapphire. If a mountainous hand could pluck this jewel from the earth it would be nestled a central piece in a breathtaking crown. A beauteous Queen decorated with a mighty realm. Such serenity intertwined with such majesty. Each precious gem sparkles with magnificent intensity. Emeralds turn toward the heat of the sun, diamonds lilt along the water. A proud spectacle. A humble elegance. Raw, unparalleled goddess, adorned with a mantle of natural righteousness and purity. Tranquil sapphire.

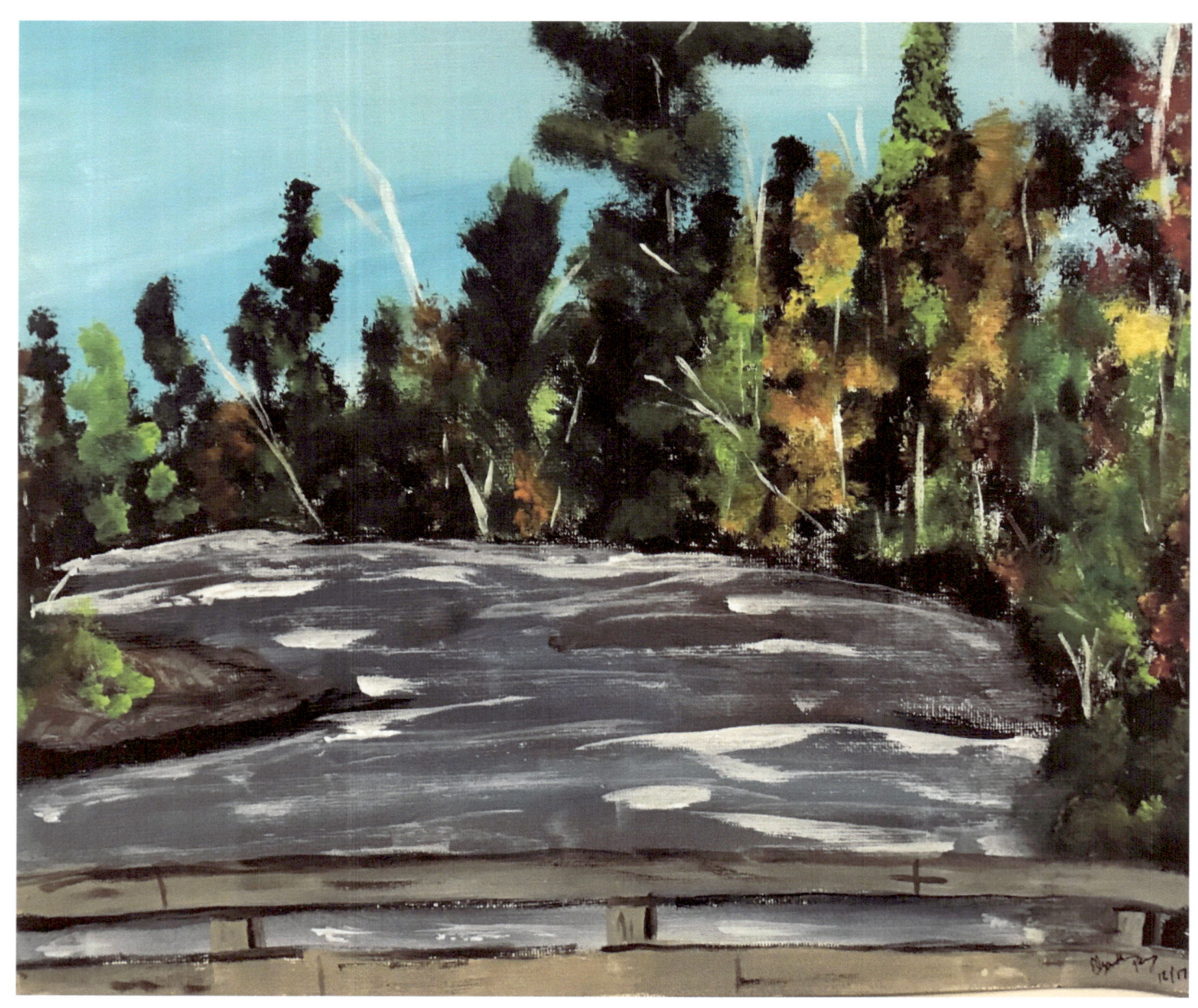

Photo for painting by Misty Thomley Wilhelm
of the Big Eric's Bridge Skanee, MI

Getting Ready

The warm autumn sun dapples the water flowing. Each leaf shivers knowing. Soon they'll all be wearing their colors of fall. Soon each silky leaf will answer the seasons call. A painting of fire will blaze along the trees tops. Every farmer ready to harvest their crops. As the water burbles beneath a bridge so the season runs its natural ridge. Walking the fine line between summer and a paint splash of autumn's golden hues. A time both ponderous and whimsical for any artist muse.

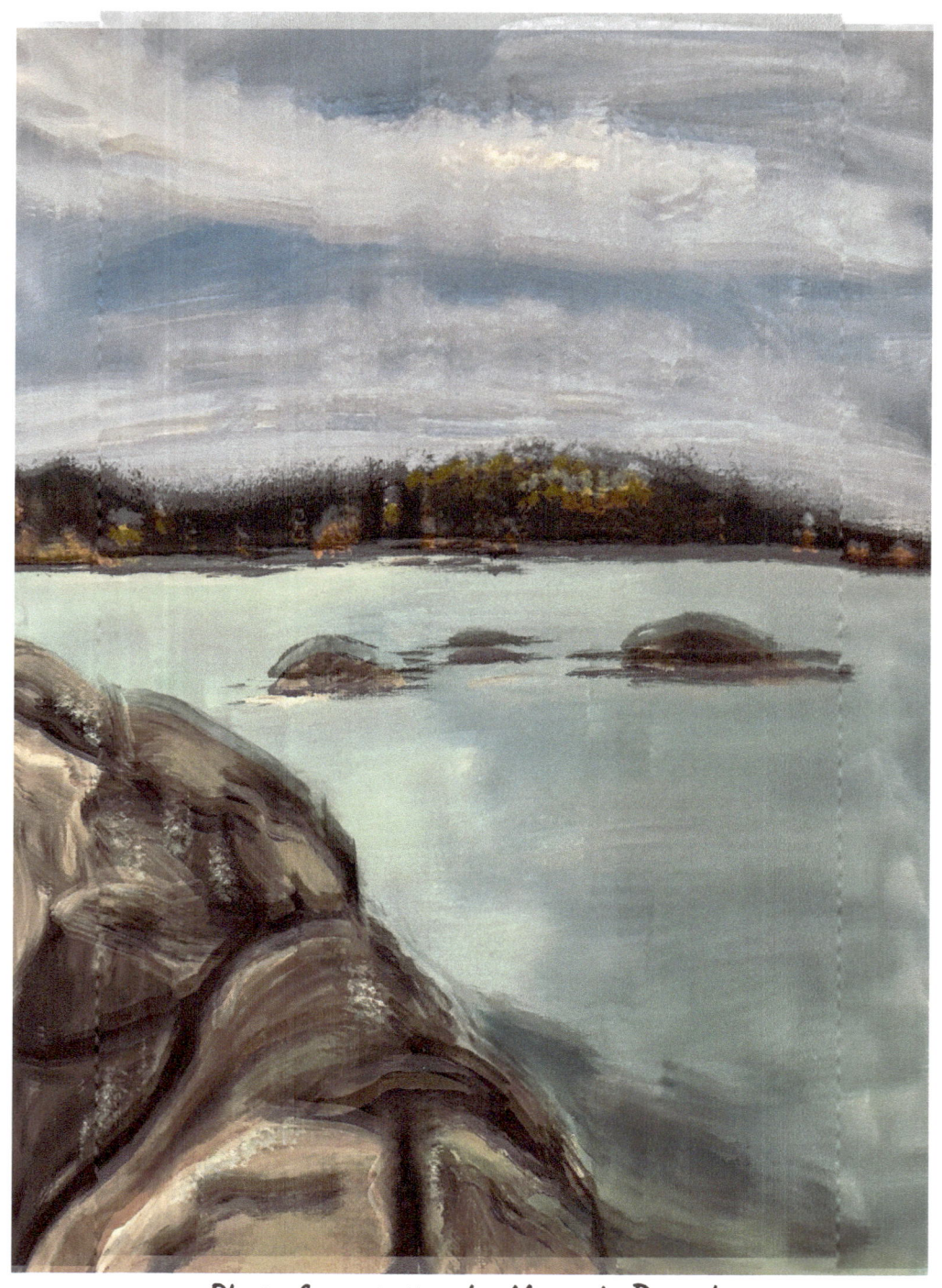

Photo for painting by Miranda Derocha
Near Marquette, MI

Deeper Than The Water

How clear the water

I can clearly see the depth

How deep is beauty?

Is strength only atop?

Or does it go deeper?

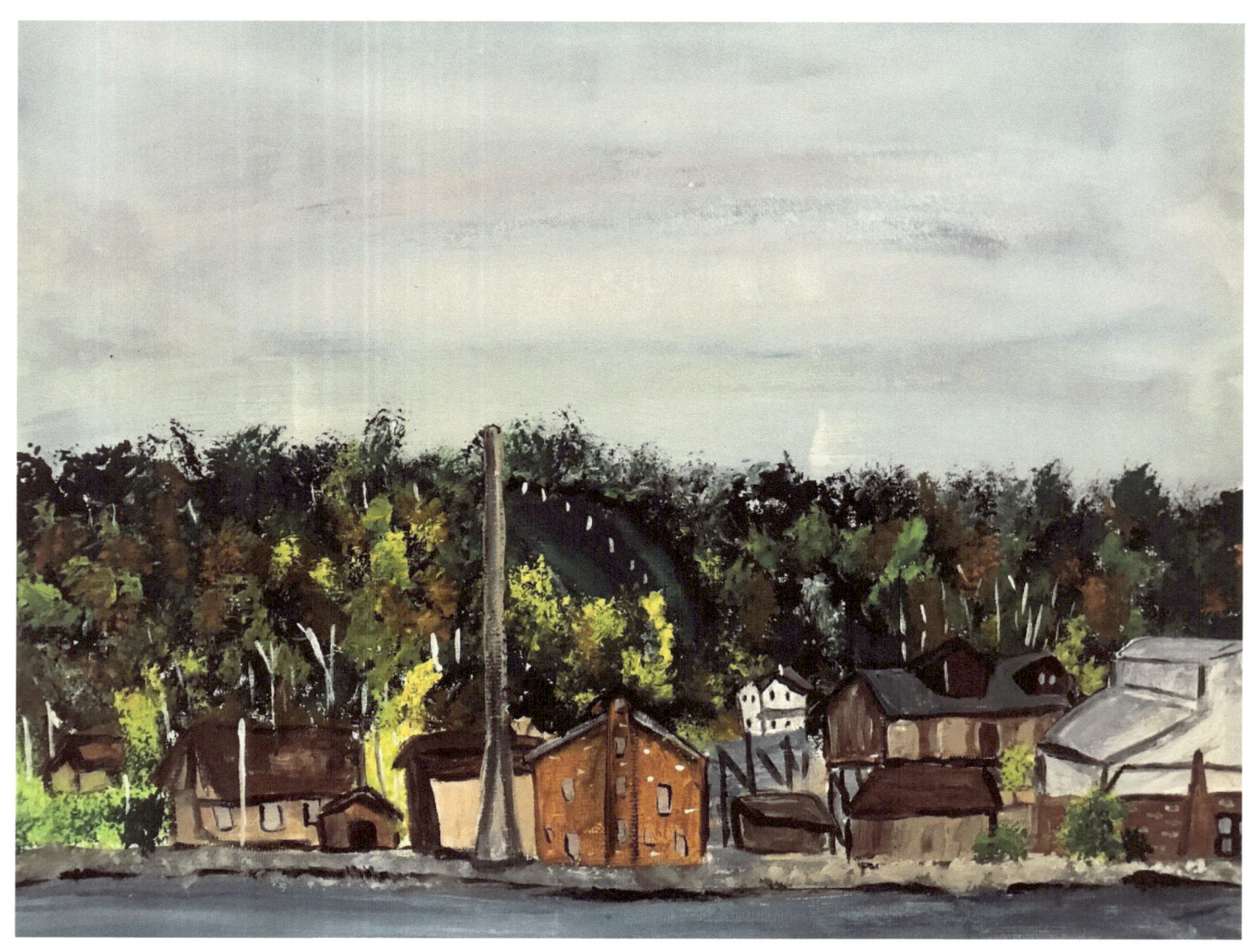

Photo for painting by Michelle Erickson Serafin
Of Bayfield, WI

Home's Call

The place where we are raised but we can't wait to get away.

The place when we are grown we wish that we could stay.

The place where we rode our bikes, played with our friends and splashed in the creek.

The place that gave that sense of home that we now all seek.

The place where our memories shine the brightest and still make our hearts glad.

The place where the good times seemed to outweigh the bad.

The place we can't go back but rather must start our own.

A new place of joy now that we are grown.

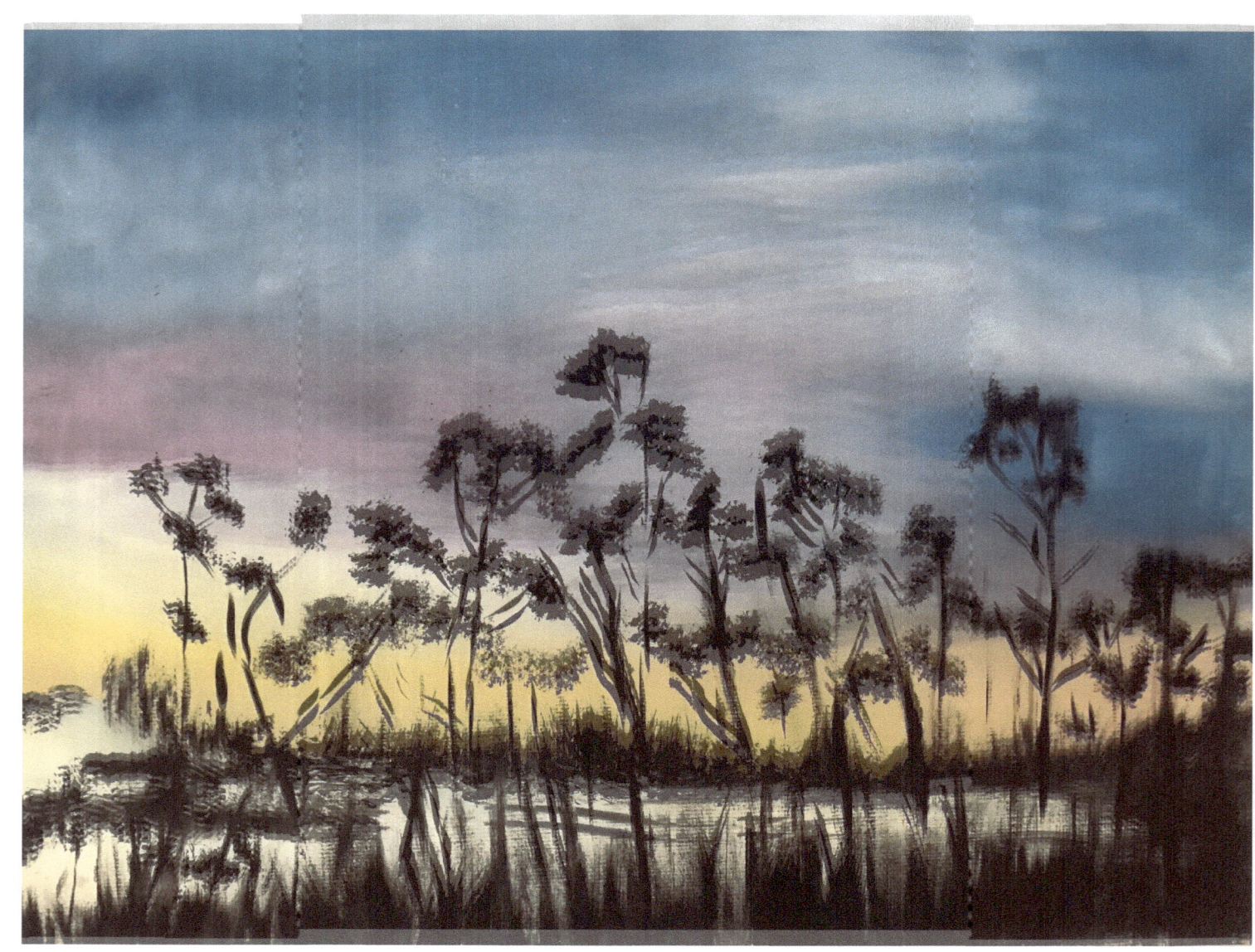

Photo for painting by Kait Keranen
Of a tansy sunset in Elo, MI

Tansy Sunset

How can something so uncomplicated be so profound? An artists brush sweeps the heavens endowing the sky with such a rich, virtuoso of colors. It glides down toward the land bringing its beautiful stream of nature's pigments where they flow and shimmer a glorious reverence to the masterpiece above. As a winters chill caresses the Earth and the glowing orb dips below the horizon, the Tansy bows its button head for an immortal slumber.

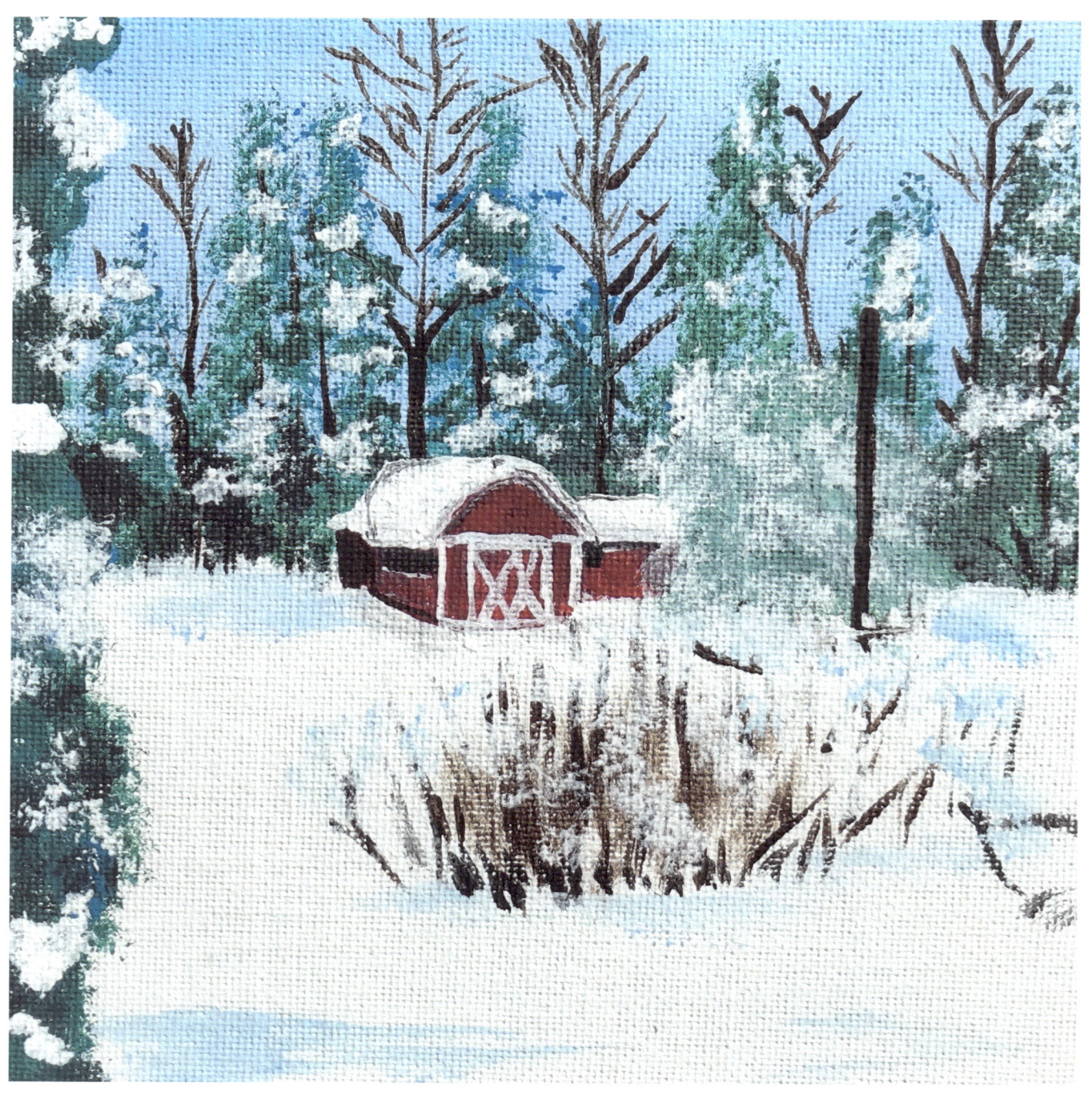

Photo for painting by Jennifer Snow
Of Cindy Massie's little red chicken coop in
Keweenaw Bay, MI

The Little Red Chicken Coop Of Keweenaw Bay

The little, red chicken coop in Keweenaw Bay

A quaint, little hut some would say

The chickens sure love it

And there it does sit

Chilled, nestled in snow

Where each feathered hen is certain to know

It's a place to come home

A place to settle after a days roam

A place to roost and nest

It's not the greatest but it is the best

That quaint little hut that some would say

That little red chicken coop in Keweenaw Bay.

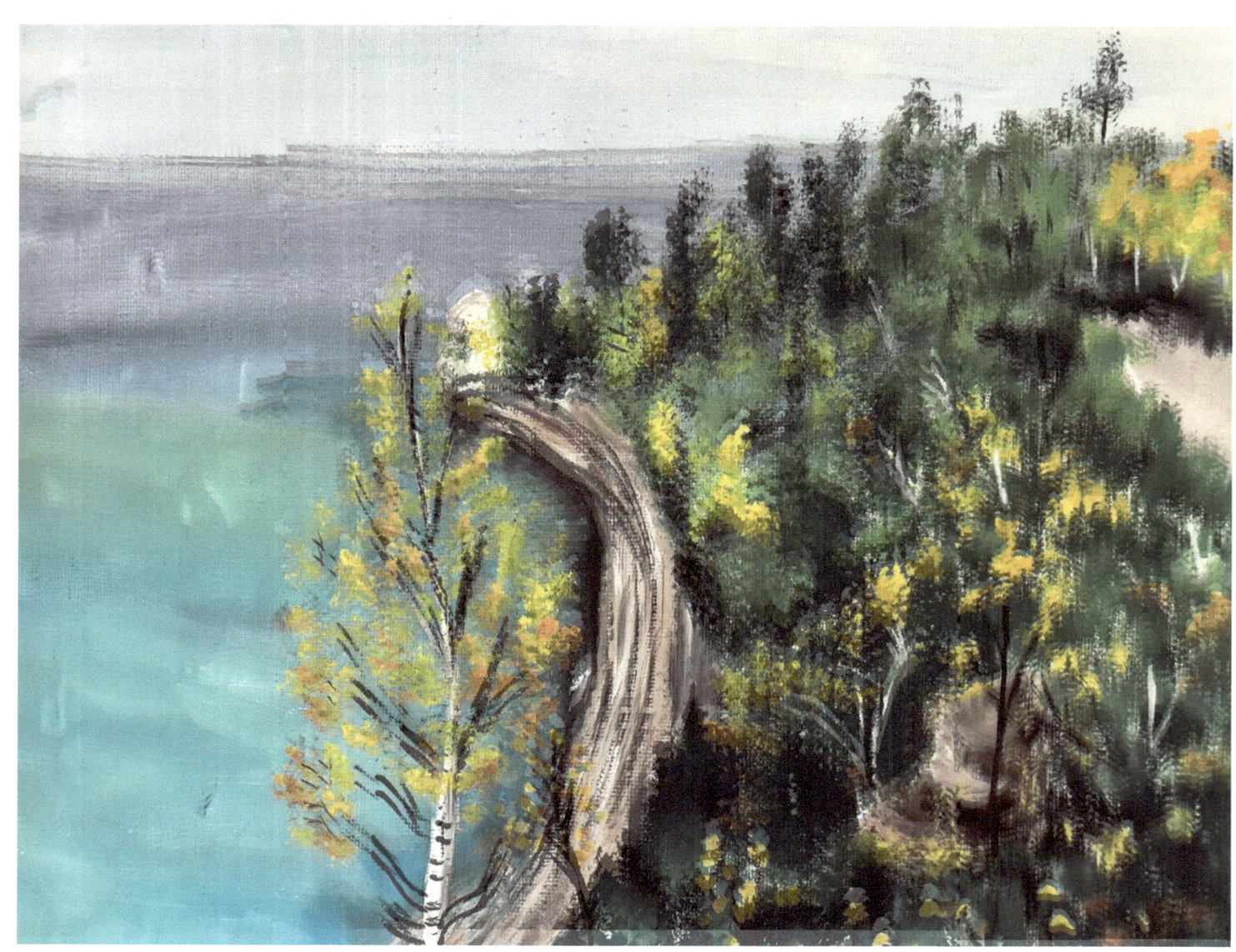

Photo for painting by Miranda Derocha
Near Marquette, MI

God's Eye View

Look down on me from on high and fill me with the serenity and peace as a birch swaying gently in an autumn breeze. Lord give me, I implore, the depth and fluidity of the Great Lake Superior; powerful enough to flow and adapt. I pray for the aged wisdom of the rocky cliffs that are kissed by the lake and listen to the whispers of the wind. Look down on this land filled with its joys and wonders and let me turn to your love and kindness just as each leaf turns itself towards the golden sun. And as the rich soil is bountiful and generous so let me be with empathy and understanding for my neighbor. Amen.

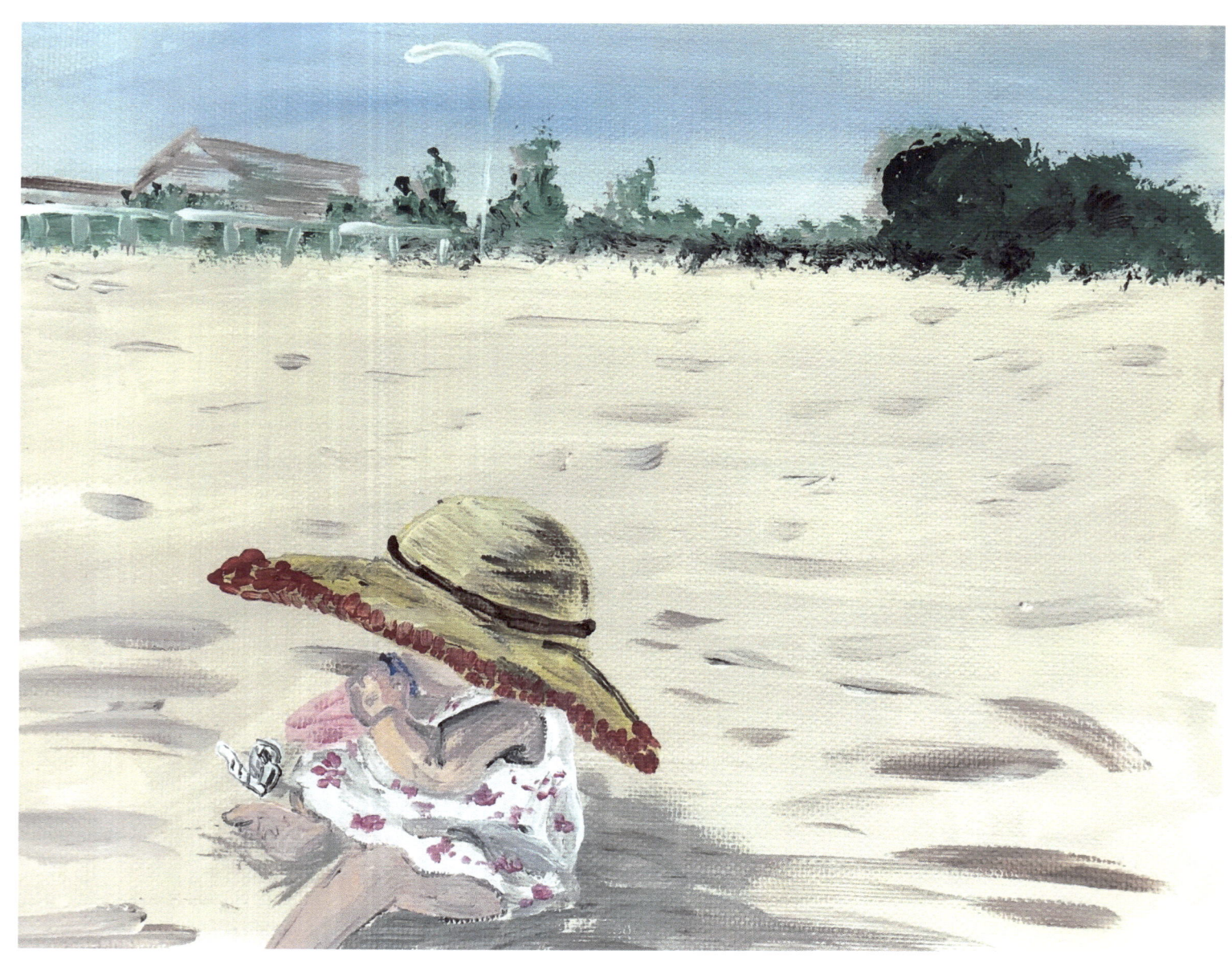

Photo for painting by Elizabeth Perry
Of her daughter Ramona Blanquera in Long Beach, MS

Baby Girl

Sifting sand between your plump fingers, how I wish this moment lingers. It seems that this busy world spins too fast and all I want is each treasured minute to last. Each tiny, precious memory is stored safely away like a treasured bauble. From when you first appeared and when you began to wobble. Across the floor and across my heart. Nothing could ever tear the two apart. I hold you in my arms, my eyes watch you grow and I hope you'll always know. No matter the distance, no matter the time. Beyond any reason or rhyme. You'll always be my baby girl.

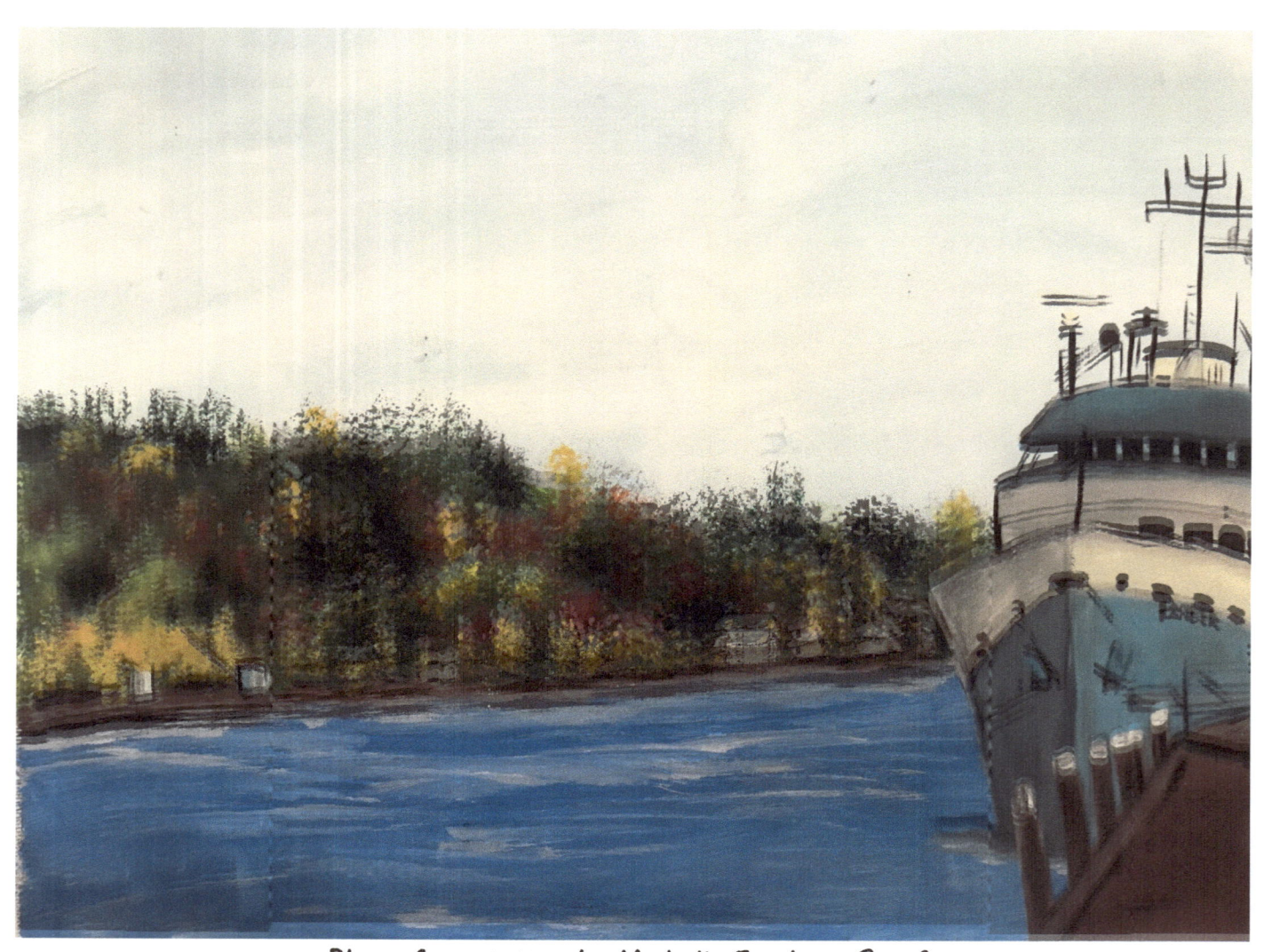

Photo for painting by Michelle Erickson Serafin
Of Bayfield, WI

Beautiful Fit

Silent sentinel

Bobbing gently in Autumn

Awaiting orders

You are contrasting

Nature abounds around you

You fit beautifully

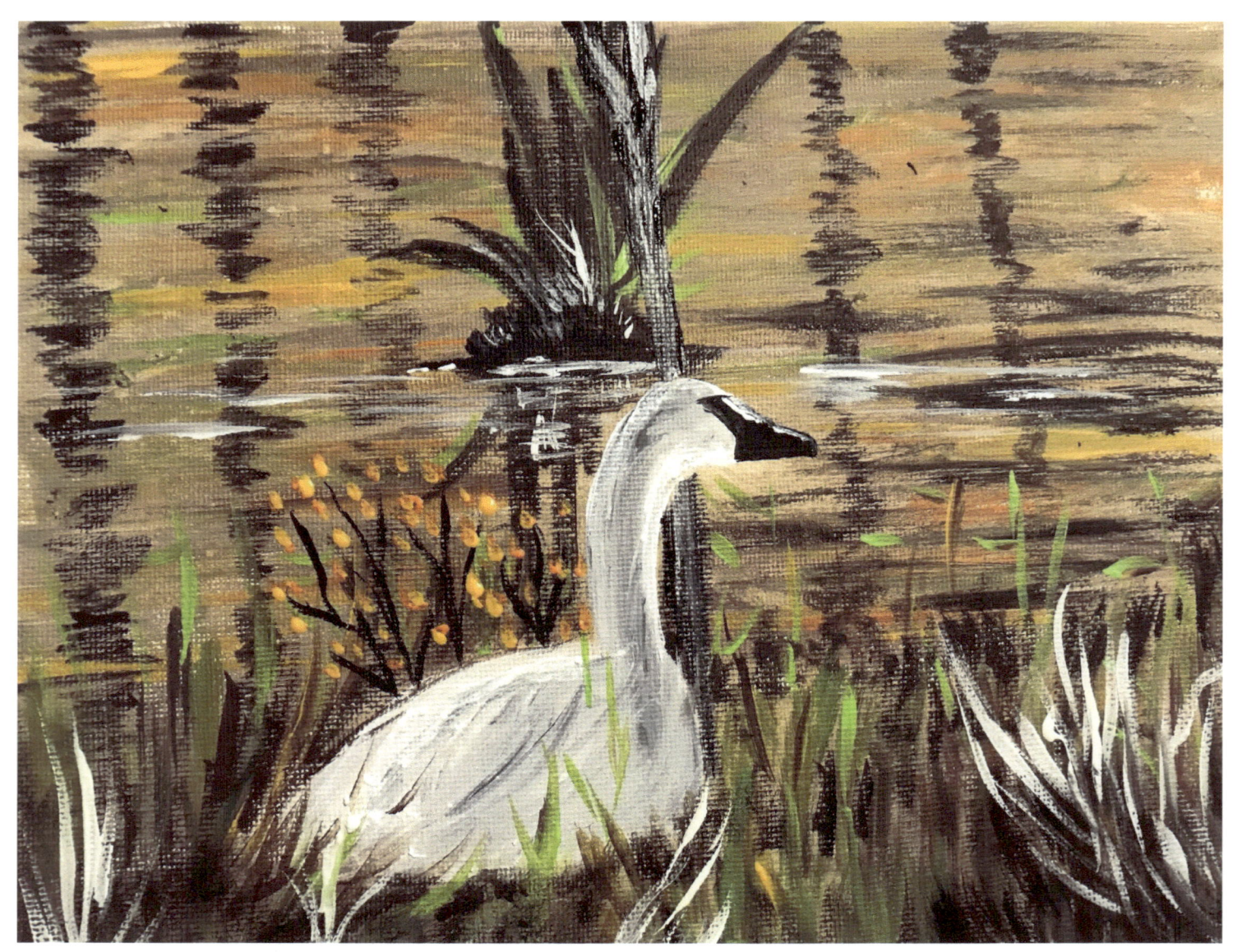

Photo for painting by Judy Thomley
Of trumpeter swan in Baraga, MI

Guardian

He stands guard awaiting his love at their shared nest

Watching closely, he'll guard his home

Peering across the pond and puffs his breast

He'll not whither, he'll not roam.

Await he shall but will she come back?

He keeps his vigil among the reeds

His faith in her will never slack

A movement there through the weeds

Is it she or perhaps a foe?

He peers closely and puffs his breast

Watching closely he must know

He'll stand guard and watch the nest.

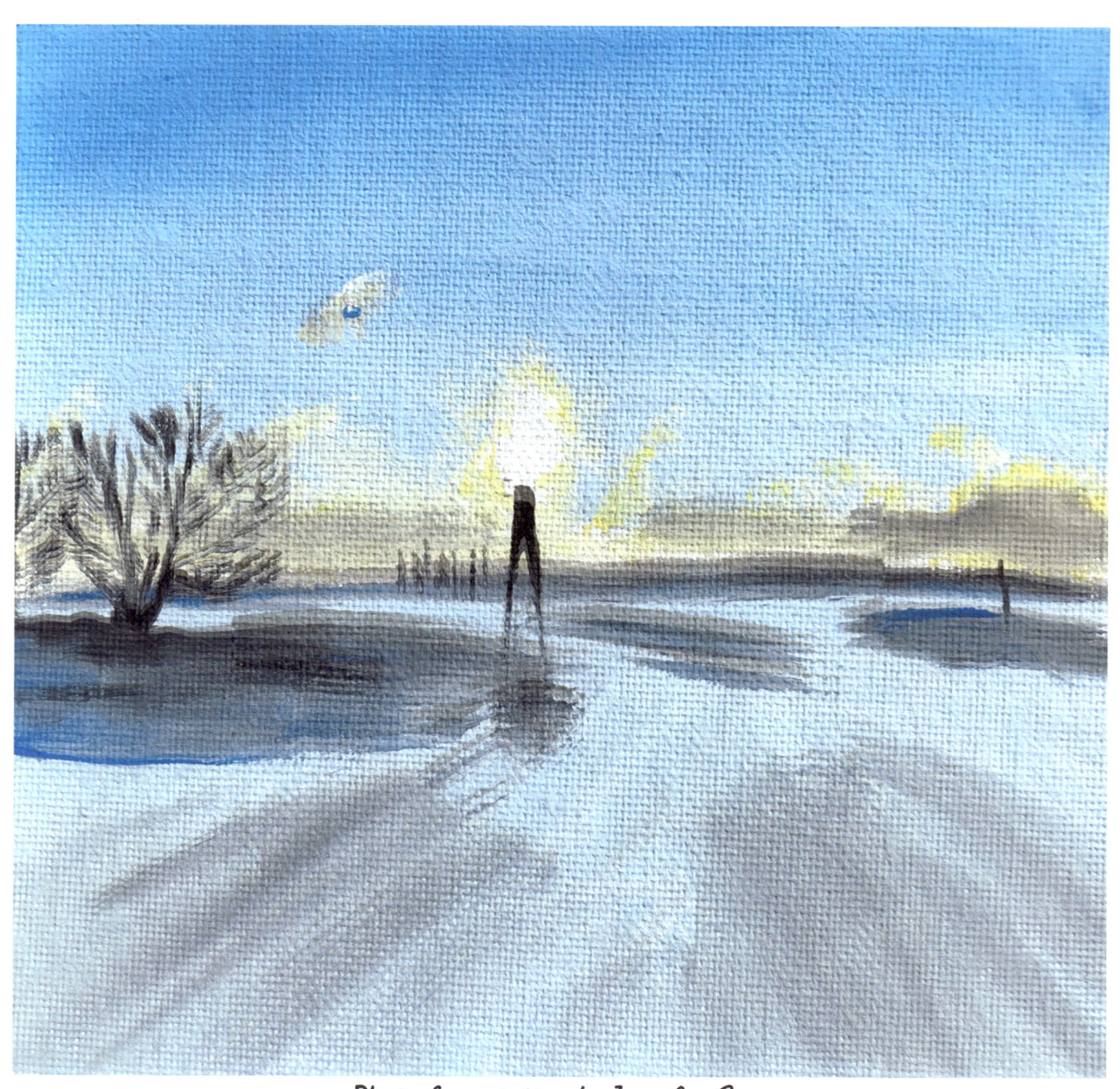

Photo for painting by Jennifer Snow
Of a sunrise in Baraga, MI

Wintry Sunrise

Bold and bright; unfurling from that deep slumber that besets each end of day. Rising over the blue hue landscape; casting lengthy shadows that reach and reach across the rolling fields of frozen crystals. Spreading tendrils of white gold into the delicate deep azure atmosphere. The globe comes to completion of one of its many, dizzying pirouettes; the maestro of seasons directs another spin and the Terra complies. Somewhere a herald adorned with a bright bouquet of feathers raucously announces the next dance and the dancers heave and sigh as they begin the steps to the newest tune.

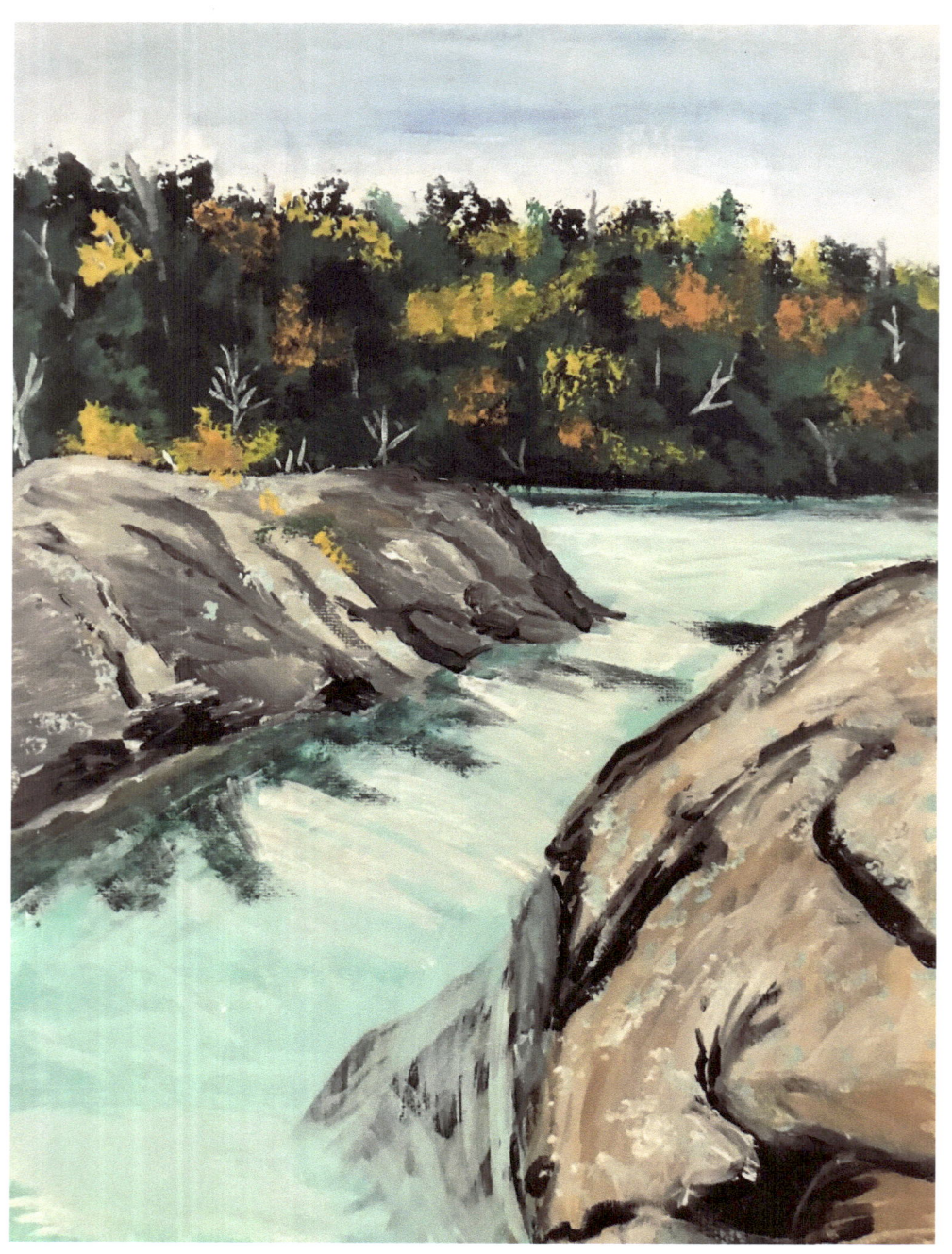

Photo for painting by Miranda Derocha
Near Marquette, MI

Which Is Mightier?

It stands a mighty boulder

As the blue green water enfolds it

And it cannot with such wit

That it thinks it is the mighty

For it does not bend and flow

And how can it conceive and know

That unmoving strength is not the greatest

But rather that which can move and change

That which can rearrange

Is a greater might than it's

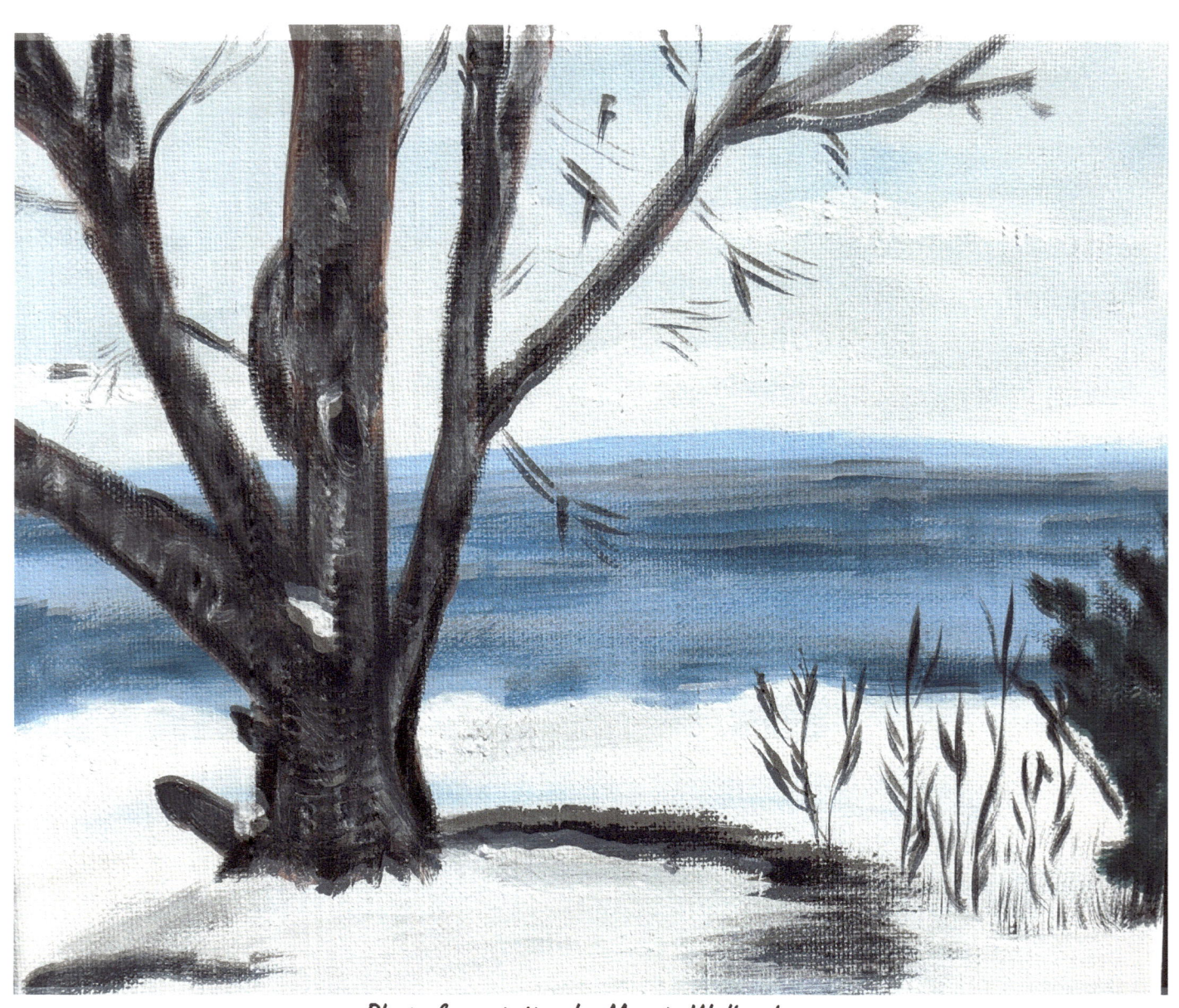

Photo for painting by Maggie Wallenslager
Of Agate Beach, MI

Not Alone

It stands alone in wintry solace. In such solitude.

But not alone

It's greenery has fallen away; they scatter the beach beneath the snow

But it does not stand alone

A kiss of sunlight, a smiling ripple of water

How can it be alone?

A neighbor of brush, a wave of a reed

No, never alone

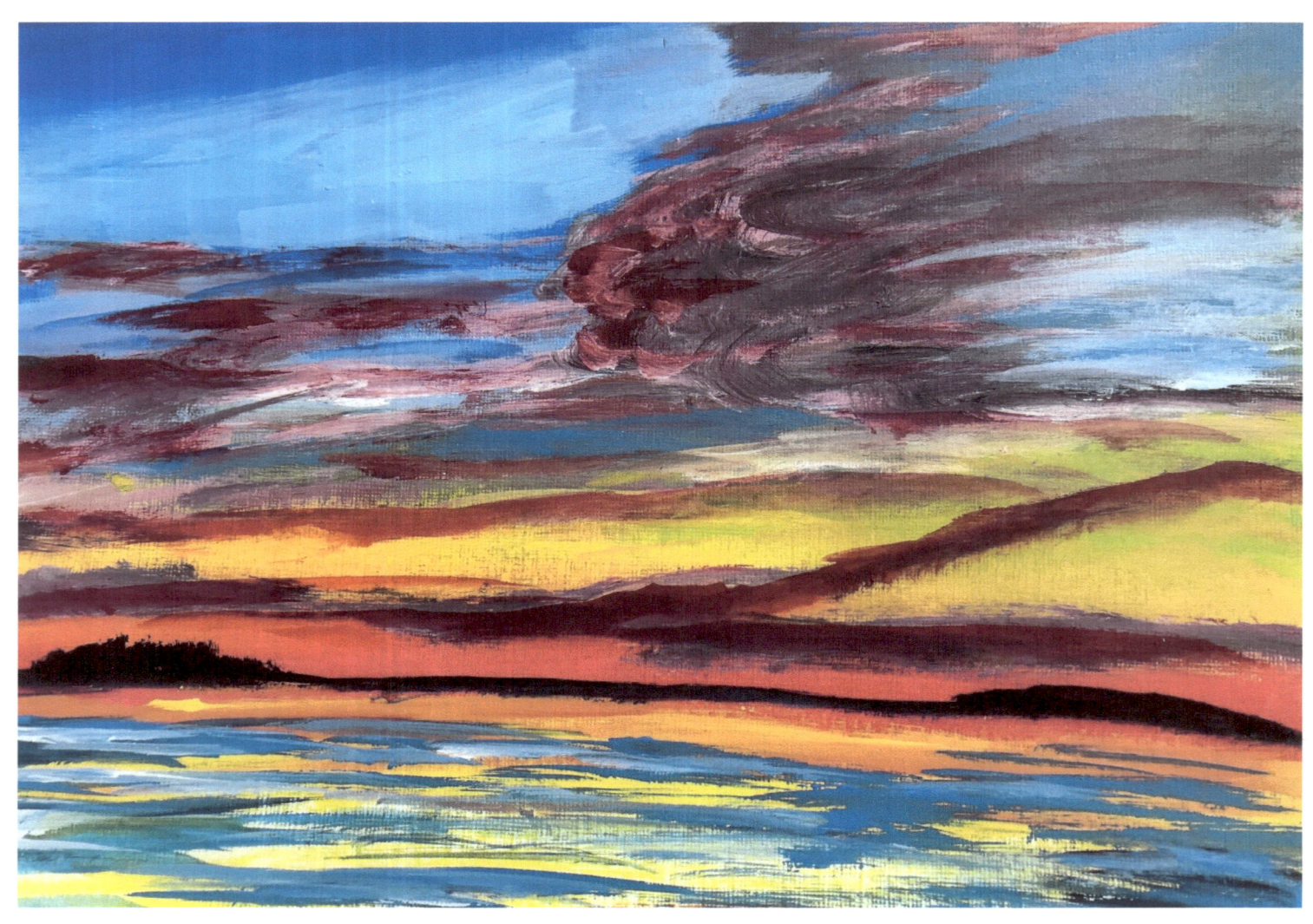

Photo for painting by Ronald Robbins
Of Crisfield, MD

The Day Is Done

The heavens are aflame!

And who is it to blame?

What fearsome hand cast the fire?

The blazing embers reaching higher!

Bits of spark alight the water!

As the flames burn ever hotter!

Twilights inky well spilling out

Will end this inferno I've no doubt

Washing down upon the raging blaze

To sizzle into a mellow haze

An announcement that the day is done

And it's time the moon replaced the sun.

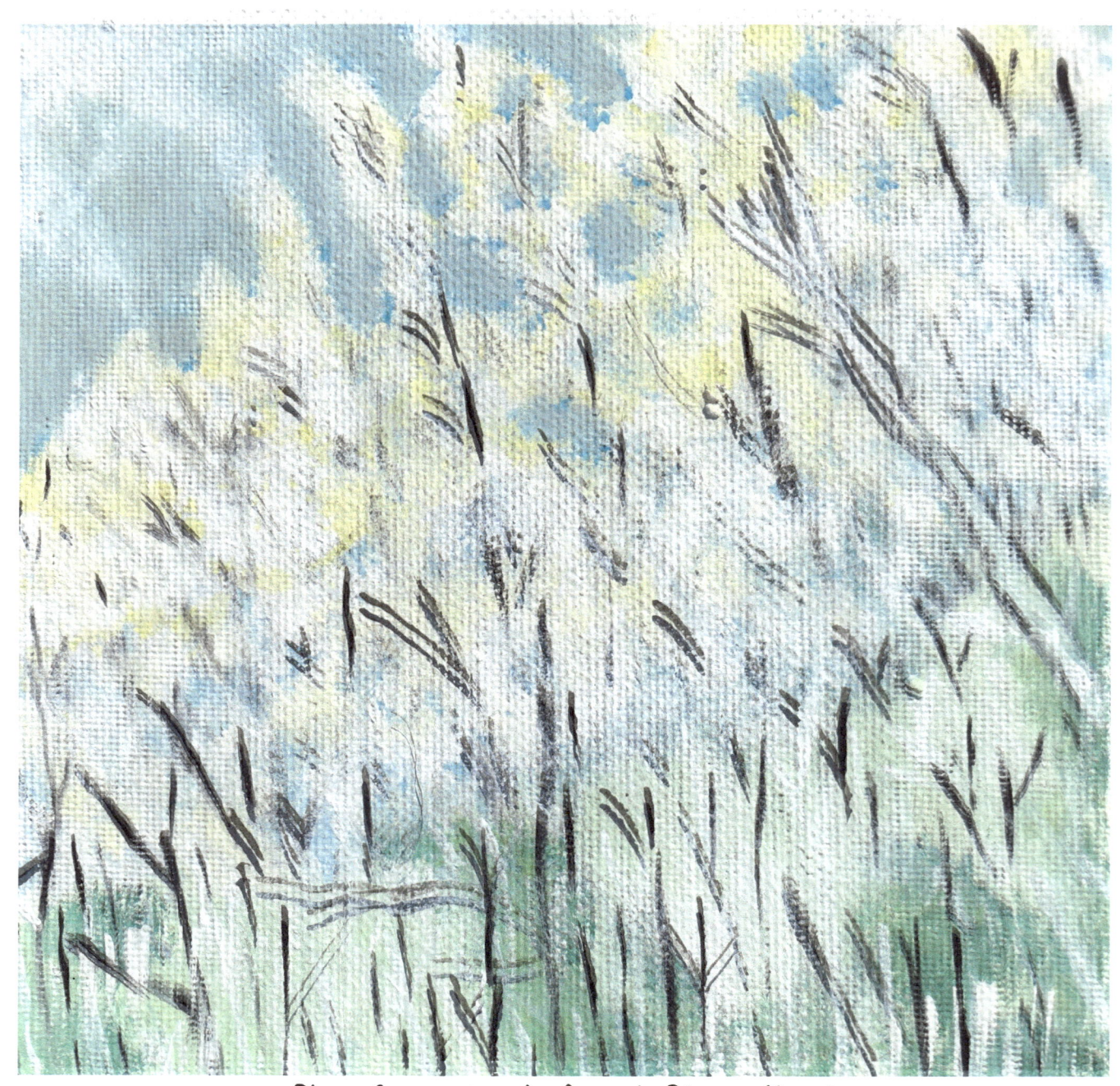

Photo for painting by Amanda Bloxton Kippola
Of the Bluff in Gladstone, MI

Dance Of Winter

How melodic is the hymn of each laden

Branch?

Heavy with the frozen ferocity of

Winter.

As the breeze whispers amongst the

Trees

Making them shiver and dance

Together

Their crystalline embellishments tinkle against one

Another

A alluring symphony of nature's

Mystique

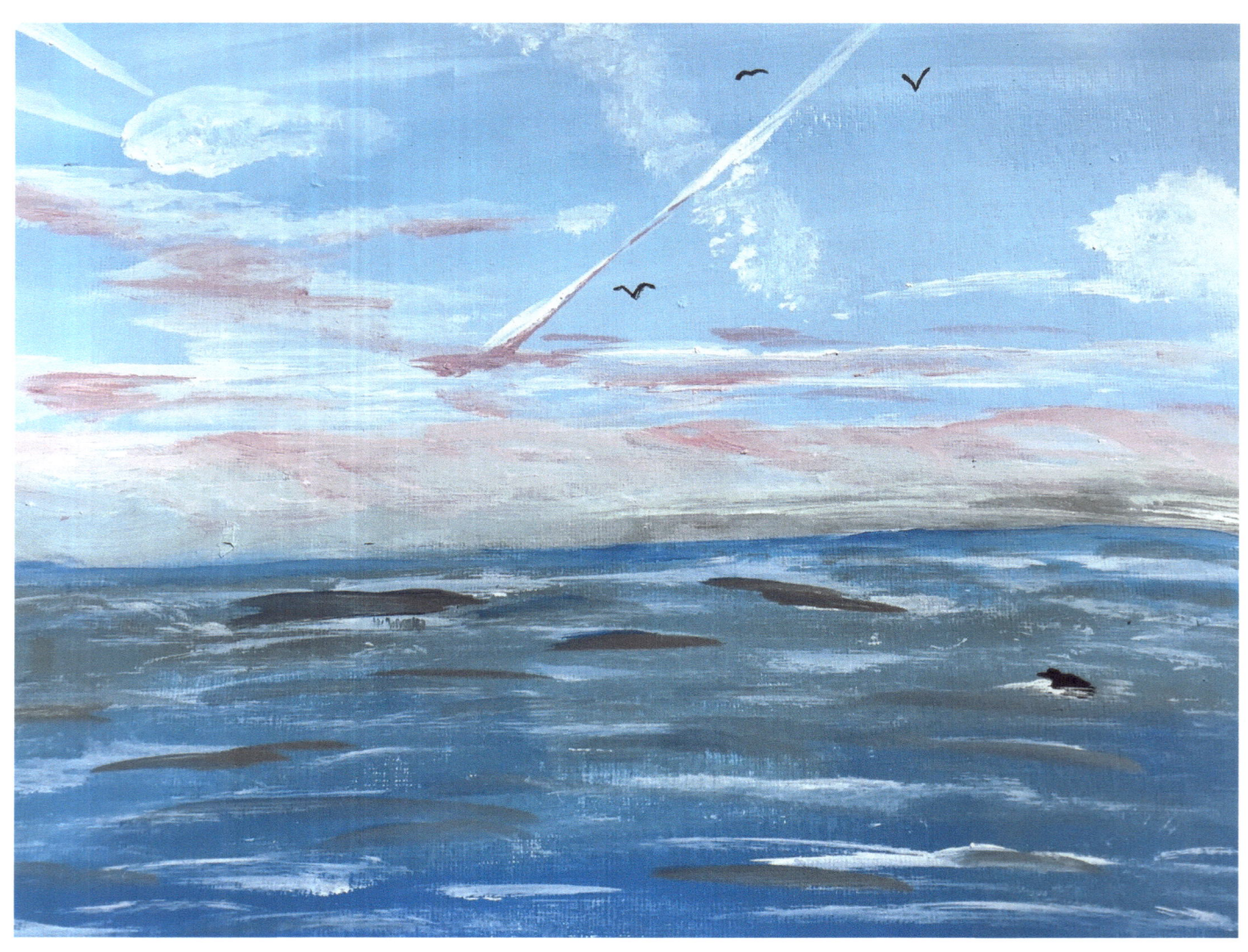

Photo for painting by Elizabeth Perry
Of Gulfport, MS

Therapy

The soft, sugary sand shifts lightly beneath me as I settle onto the slightly cool beach. It is only February after all. As I sit upon the shore, I dig my toes into the warm but slightly cool sand. Since it is only February, though the weather is lovely, I am alone on the beach. Alone except for the gulls and pelicans that search overhead for a meal in the waters below. Alone, except for the little sandpipers running after each little wave. Alone except for the thoughts that fill my mind to overflowing: projects, money, deadlines, children, relationships…each of these vie for a spot in my mind. But that's why I came here, to this place of quiet. To be surrounded, not by the hustle and bustle of so called civilization, but rather the busyness of nature. The busyness is calming. It highlights what's truly important. It creates perspective. So I sit here on this quiet beach, gazing out at a blue sky streaked with the pink of a setting sun, and I drink it in. I allow it to quiet my mind and fill my soul.

www.ingramcontent.com/pod-product-compliance
Lightning Source LLC
Chambersburg PA
CBHW051935210526
45473CB00006B/2254